STRONG SPIRIT

HOPE FOR WOMEN LIVING WITH ILLNESS

Holly Dickson-Ramos

Cover Design — Kerry Dickson Design & Consulting
Editors — Lynn Smith, Brooke Ramos Dickson, Andrea Butcher-Milne

Photo Credits: All photos courtesy of www.pixabay.com.

All quotations used by permission of author:
Carnes, Micah, www.madebyacarpenter.wordpress.com
Faulds, Bethany, "The Chronic Cross: Understanding Chronic Illness
Through The Cross of Jesus"

The content of this book is not intended to be a substitute
for professional medical advice, diagnosis, or treatment. Always seek
the advice of your physician or other qualified health provider
with any questions you may have regarding a medical condition.

ISBN-13: 978-1-7774225-0-9 (paperback)
ISBN-13: 978-1-7774225-1-6 (e-book)

I dedicate this book
to my husband, Alexis.
When we made our vows
you didn't know
your lively, youthful bride
would get sick
and stay sick.
Your love and loyalty
infuse life with warmth
and comfort.
Your patience and gentleness
when I am grumpy, weak, or struggling
help me keep going.
God uses you in my life
to show me how deeply
He loves me.

TABLE OF CONTENTS

STRONG SPIRIT
Hope for Women Living With Illness

---

*F*ew of us expect to be seriously ill. Fifteen years ago I thought that perfect health and carefree days were the norm.

In my early thirties, I felt energized and capable… until one day my body failed me.

In the years that followed I realized that real women struggle. Real women are not like shiny ads, radiating beauty, good spirits and perfect health every day.

For many of us, life is complicated. Challenging. We battle illness, longing for many things: to be loved, to live meaningful lives, to enjoy just one day without symptoms, without triggering a condition, to feel capable of nurturing our loved ones the way we want to, to be defined not by a condition or a diagnosis, but by our inner selves — the person God sees when He looks at us.

In the pages that follow I'll share some of the highs and lows of my own journey and I'll introduce you to women who wrestle with chronic pain, cancer, anxiety, depression, and other conditions that have impacted their physical and emotional well-being.

You and I belong to a community of real women who suffer and struggle — although brokenness may be part of this season of our lives, let's inspire one another to find God's deeper purpose for us as we allow Him to use our strengths and our weakness for His glory.

1

STRUGGLE

After you have suffered for a little while, the God of all grace,
who called you to His eternal glory in Christ,
will Himself perfect, confirm, strengthen and establish you.
1 PETER 5:10 (NASB)

The lowest point in my life with illness came a few months after an unsuccessful cardiac ablation. I went forward, one Sunday, to be anointed and prayed over by church elders. We called on God together, asking Him for healing.

God heard our prayers and intervened in the lives of those who came forward, but not in the way we expected Him to. We hoped for immediate physical healing and this did not happen.

I felt angry with God for ignoring our plea and I wondered if prayer made any difference at all. I asked myself if God even existed.

Then one morning, as I read my Bible, I noticed that John the Baptist went through a similar struggle. Even though John was really close to Jesus, when life didn't turn out how John wanted (when he found himself in prison for no good reason) he began to wonder if Jesus was really who He claimed to be *(Matthew 11:2-3)*. Just like me.

It's a common response to suffering, I've realized: doubt about God's existence and character.

Deep inside, in the places where I am disappointed with life, where I suffer from ongoing pain and wrestle with emotional trauma, I have tantrum after mental tantrum because life is not as

3

fun as I want it to be. I don't *want* to suffer. I don't *deserve* to suffer. I shouldn't *have* to suffer. I am entitled to happiness. Aren't we all?

I *thought* we were until I ran across the verse from 1 Peter that begins this chapter. Read it again, and then tell me if it doesn't suggest that *struggle* is vital to the faith-filled life; *suffering* may be the prerequisite for strong faith.

After reading this verse I realized that God's purpose for my life is not unfettered fun. He is perfecting me for another life in another place and the process might not be entirely painless.

I'm not suggesting that God caused my condition. I know that because of all the wrong choices humanity has made throughout centuries we live in an imperfect world. There can't be free will without the possibility of suffering. I see that.

But couldn't He keep this pain from touching *me*? And everyone I love?

He could if He wanted to.

But that's me forgetting to think of this moment in context; this moment is a sentence in a paragraph in a chapter in a book.

The book of my life has a sad section — the sick section. These pages document the struggle.

But I'm chasing hope, so I've peeked at the ending of my story. *This* season is just a chapter in my book. *This moment* is not all there is. For you or for me.

Life will seem less bleak if we keep the larger narrative in mind and hold fast to Peter's words. Suffering and death are not absolute evils to be avoided at all costs. Jesus himself had to suffer and die to save us, a sad chapter in His story, but essential to that final, victorious end.

In this fallen world most people will have to suffer at some point to some degree, but God promises to use it for good, if we let Him.

Let's do our best to re-frame pain in a context that gives it meaning. **We have not been rejected or abandoned by God.**

I believe that God, with the heart of a loving father, cries with us and gives us an opportunity like the one He gave Job — to trust Him and to embrace His nearness when we're hurting.

No one likes to suffer, and I will not pretend I don't want healing in my life. I do.

But that initial crisis of faith has passed. I choose to trust.

PRAYER

Loving God,
increase my faith.
On days when You seem distant and uncaring,
remind me of these truths:
that You created me for a reason,
that You have been near to me each moment of my life,
that You use suffering to shape me
and to remind me of my need for You,
that You are not indifferent to the pain of this broken world;
that You are not indifferent to my pain.
Draw me close during my hardest moments;
may these times fuse my spirit to Yours;
may my suffering be the glue that bonds me to You —
my Creator,
the One who rescues me.

Meet
ANDREA

CHALLENGE: Multiple Sclerosis

IN THE BEGINNING

When I first was diagnosed with MS I had pretty much lost the use of my legs. Every morning when I woke up, I asked God to restore my legs to me. If that wasn't in His plan for the day, could He at least make my life purposeful to others? What a plan He had for me! He set me on a path of volunteering for some amazing organizations. I have had relationships and experiences that I would never have had if I wasn't diagnosed. The phrase "When I got busy, I got better" comes to mind.

DAY TO DAY CHALLENGES

I experience numbness, pins and needles, sensory overload in busy situations, fatigue, inability to walk long distances and an overactive bladder. My biggest challenge with MS is to focus on the here and now, not what the future has in store for me.

HOW I COPE

I am strict with daily routine. I try to wake and go to bed at the same time every day. I follow an ebb and flow for my day to make sure that I don't get too fatigued. I am strict with my medication, food, treadmill and physiotherapy routines. I set achievable long term goals. I attend church and Bible study regularly. I believe in living a well-balanced life, taking care of my emotional, physical and spiritual needs.

ABOUT FINANCES

I haven't had what one would call a normal work life, and this has impacted my family's financial life. But I've found that God provides. We have a roof over our heads, food on the table and we do enjoy regular vacations. What more could I want from life?

SPECIAL PEOPLE

God has placed a sisterhood in Christ around me. I have had close, supportive relationships with women who have strong faith in God and who come around me to teach me His word. I want to acknowledge Angela Maxwell for being my godmother when I was baptized in my thirties. She has always been a strong teacher, mentor and cheerleader in my life.

LAST THOUGHTS

I do believe this has bought me closer to God. I ask Him on a regular basis to help me help others. I feel blessed to be used this way. I see His hand in the pathways that have been opened for me but I also see His hand in the doors that have been closed. He has taught me to be patient in understanding where I'm meant to be at any given time in my life. I'm not great at remembering Bible verses but I feel God's presence around me on my life's journey.

PAIN

O LORD, hear me as I pray;
pay attention to my groaning.
Listen to my cry for help, my King and my God.
PSALM 5:1-2

*I*n college I ripped a ligament while charging across an unkept football field in the dark. My knee doubled in size and gave out for weeks afterwards, even when the initial pain had subsided.

Sometimes I think sustaining an injury that caused months of pain, a lengthy rehab, learning to sleep in new positions, and asking my roommate to help put my clothes on gave me a tiny taste of what chronic illness would be like later in life.

Physical pain was part of recovery from knee surgery in my early twenties, and it is part of my life today.

Not everyone wrestling with illness faces ongoing pain, but many do, and those who don't may struggle with other physical discomfort triggered by emotional distress. In any case, **pain, whether emotional or physical, is hard.**

Chronic pain saps the strength and crushes the spirit. It's traumatic. Although you can talk to others about pain, no one feels exactly what you feel, so pain can be lonely.

Often, pain causes us to struggle with hard questions: *Why does God continue to allow this? Why did it happen in the first place? How can a sovereign God, who is able to heal, leave us to deal with a crippling loss of abilities or horrible experience of pain?*

Pain is real and suffering is hard. Most of us would not choose this path. If it were possible, most of us would compel God to fix the brokenness in our lives. This desire for healing, I've noticed, can be distracting. While *we* focus on these unresolved details of our lives, wishing God would bring us the miraculous healing we know He is capable of, *His* priority continues to be our *spiritual* well-being. I find it hard to shift my view from the temporary to the eternal, but well worth the effort. In doing so, I'm able to put my desire for healing on the back burner, focusing, instead, on the lessons I'm learning from the temporary trials I face.

INSIGHT & EMPATHY

Anyone who has suffered can look back and see that dark days seed in us insights that would never grow during carefree times. Although we may long for a different self (one blissfully unaware of the tedious grind of pain) or a different life (one free from undeserved hardship), our experiences equip us to comfort others. We've suffered. We know what it's like to struggle, not just with something fleeting or ordinary, but with something persistent and intense. This gives us a unique ability to empathize with others who suffer.

INTIMACY WITH GOD

Perhaps the most notable thing about pain is its tendency to drive us to God. Suffering alone and in silence may seem admirable if you're watching an old Western, but it isn't healthy and most of us need to reach out beyond ourselves for support and comfort. Other people who come around us in life can be a beautiful source of encouragement (evidence of this is the heartfelt gratitude expressed by the women whose stories appear in this book — all of them are so grateful for those special people God has placed in their lives). But people cannot be with us in each hard moment. God can. **There is no better way to face pain than allowing it to drive us into God's presence.**

The next time you feel the tug of sadness and self-pity inviting you to compare yourself to the glossy, smiling image of others inhabiting your mind, push aside the lie that "normal" means pain-free and the idea that God loves happy people the most.

Scripture reveals to us God's heart for the humble, for those who suffer, and for those experiencing loss. *1 Peter 4* describes a counter-cultural faith — a movement that calls adherents to suffering and hardship, not prosperity, fame or happiness.

That's our God. He opposes the proud and gives grace to the humble *(1 Peter 5:5)*.

Our gaping need, our inability to fix our bodies or our spirits here in this fallen world reveals to us that we are not self-sufficient. We need God. Joni Eareckson Tada calls suffering "the sheepdog that chases us into God's presence" — the place all of us are meant to seek out and settle in.

Meet
RUTHIE

CHALLENGES: Incest Survivor, Obesity, Anxiety, Depression, Breast Cancer Survivor

IN THE BEGINNING

My physical challenges date back to when I experienced incest as a child. We had a foster brother in our home who came from a difficult background and demonstrated sexual dysfunction. I was quite young at the time, so don't recall if my parents were aware of what was going on behind the closed doors of the house. I was too afraid to speak out.

When I was thirteen, my Mom took me to have a physical with a doctor she'd been seeing. The doctor had put my Mom on a strict diet, and she had lost over one hundred pounds. I believe my Mom was concerned that I'd gain weight like she had. I had a few extra pounds on before going into grade nine. This appointment was traumatic for me. I wasn't prepared for the physical, particularly the pap smear. I also wasn't prepared for the doctor's "talk" with me. I clearly remember him stating, *"Don't you know boys don't like fat girls?"* I was very hurt by this statement.

ANOTHER CHALLENGE

After my biological brother died of AIDS at age thirty-two, I was heartbroken. His death and the subsequent end to my first marriage were triggers that caused a serious depressive episode. Suicidal thoughts and a complete inability to function caused my doctor to recommend Homewood

Health Centre, a comprehensive psychiatric hospital, to me. There, I understood I hadn't really grieved the loss of my brother; I learned about emotional colour blindness and how feelings are often suppressed after traumatic events. It was at Homewood that I confessed the childhood incest to the medical team. The hospital chaplain and I had some good long talks about Christianity and my own confused beliefs and feelings. Within a year of discharge from the hospital, I accepted Jesus into my heart and was baptised. My new life in Christ had begun!

DAY TO DAY STRUGGLES

Obesity has caused many challenges in my life. I've spent considerable energy beating myself up for my gluttony and calling out to God to help me overcome this condition. Over the years, obesity has caused my joints to inflame and at age sixty-four, I needed a knee replacement. Obesity has affected the intimacy I want with my husband of thirty years. It has affected my self-worth.

HOW I COPE

Obesity, depression and anxiety have been treated through medical doctors, counsellors, adherence to Weight Watchers (my AA) and most importantly, through prayer and time in the Word. I continue to be on an anti-depressant to assist with my highs and lows.

Good counsellors and our almighty Counsellor have taught me to recognize ALL my emotions, the full rainbow that God has given us. These include the positive emotions like love and joy, as well as the difficult emotions like anger, grief and sorrow. I have learned to recognize difficult emotions and hand them over to God. I walk with God every hour of every day of my life asking Him to intervene and give me the courage to experience authentic emotion instead of suppressing what I'm feeling.

When days become particularly bleak, I tend to oversleep and overeat. I combat this negative cycle by praying, writing in my journal, spending time in the Word, and talking to loving and wise friends. Eating nutritionally and spending time outside walking and enjoying God's creation also help a lot.

Depression and anxiety are terrible demons. Thanks to my reliance on Jesus, I have not suffered another significant depressive episode requiring hospitalization; however, there have been seasons in my life I've really needed to spend more time with the Lord to regain the peace He provides.

ABOUT INTIMACY

As mentioned earlier, obesity and depression affect the intimacy I share with my husband. I love my husband dearly. We are both in our second marriage and vow to love each other until the Lord calls us home. My husband has his own demons to battle. Our demons can cause a rift in our relationship on a physical and intimate level. We work hard at our marriage and ask God to be in our lives on a daily basis. Our commitment to one another is strong.

SPIRITUAL GROWTH

A very meaningful scripture passage for me is *Romans 5: 1-5*.

> Therefore, since we have been made right in God's sight by faith, we have peace with God because of what Jesus Christ our Lord has done for us. Because of our faith, Christ has brought us into this place of undeserved privilege where we now stand, and we confidently and joyfully look forward to sharing God's glory.

> We can rejoice, too, when we run into problems and trials, for we know that they help us develop

endurance. And endurance develops strength of character, and character strengthens our confident hope of salvation. And this hope will not lead to disappointment. For we know how dearly God loves us, because he has given us the Holy Spirit to fill our hearts with his love.

The Holy Spirit led me to these verses as I recovered from serious depression at age thirty-two. At that time, the Homewood hospital chaplain was instrumental in encouraging me to find my way back to Jesus, and another pastor asked me directly, *"What is your relationship with Jesus?"* No one had ever asked me that before! That same pastor and his wife led me to Jesus, and I was baptised when I was thirty-three years old. Praise Him!

Since that time, I have leaned heavily on the Lord because He is my strength, my refuge, and my hope in times of trouble. He has blessed my husband and me so richly. We didn't have children in our first marriages, but so desired them. We were able to have two children in our thirties. We now have three gorgeous grandchildren! God exceeds our expectations!

A MEANINGFUL VERSE

Yet those who wait for the LORD will gain new strength; they will mount up with wings like eagles, they will run and not get tired, they will walk and not become weary. (Isaiah 40:31)

In 2009 I was diagnosed with stage three breast cancer. During the surgeries, chemotherapy, radiation and Herceptin infusions, I was truly at peace. I could envision myself tucked under eagle's wings. *Isaiah 40:31* kept coming into my heart.

SPECIAL PEOPLE

Next to Jesus, my family is my earthly inspiration. My husband, James, is a strong protector and our children, Lindsay and Robert, along with their families, multiply our joy over and over. There have been pastors, doctors, counsellors and so many good, good loving friends who have supported me over the years. My faith community at Willow Creek Baptist Church has been instrumental in my spiritual and mental health for over twenty years. Praise God for them!

ALREADY NOT YET

For in Him we live and move and exist.
ACTS 17:28

*G*od created me, and in Him I live and move and take each breath. His nearness comforts me. His unconditional love anchors me. His promises give me hope. I am His and He is mine and this is the central relationship of my being, of my life.

This certainty about God's goodness wavered a bit, though, when I got sick, stayed sick and prayer did not result in my miraculous healing.

Why would He choose to heal others, but not me?

I spent a few years wrestling with this question, trying to work out an understanding of the scriptures in light of the fact that many prayers offered in faith are not answered as we want them to be.

The phrase **already not yet** is one I've come to appreciate. It's short, simple, and it captures the idea that we live in an in-between time. Christ has completed His work on the cross — we have been rescued from our sin; this is the **already** part of the phrase. But we live in a fallen world and we see the effects of this everywhere. The fulfillment of all God has planned for us has not yet come to be; this is the **not yet** part.

Settling into an intellectual understanding of this theological idea has been helpful.

But what really quieted my angst-ridden, why-driven inner tantrums were the lyrics of a song. My thoughtful sister sent me a song and as the words and music filled my little car on a familiar country road, I wept. All of the mental noise haunting me was replaced with one question: *Will you still be His, even if you lose it all?*

That I could answer.

I will.

I believe that God is good. He cares about our suffering. He could not stand to see a world set on an uninterrupted path of self-destruction. He intervened. He sent His son, Jesus.

No one explains this better than Bethany Faulds, in my opinion. Bethany struggles with pain and other symptoms due to a chronic condition and she has given me permission to share her thoughts on illness and the cross with you.

THE CHRONIC CROSS: UNDERSTANDING CHRONIC ILLNESS THROUGH THE CROSS OF JESUS
by Bethany Faulds

God's self-giving love gives the chronically ill lasting hope that is deeper than the physical healing of this world. Looking to the cross, the chronically ill may confidently proclaim "God hates my illness!" Looking to the resurrection, the chronically ill may trumpet "God has freed me from my illness!" The chronically ill live in the tension of the already-not-yet quality of this age. Christ has already won the victory — they may rest assured that one day "He will wipe away every tear from their eyes, and death shall be no more, neither shall there be mourning, nor crying, nor pain anymore, for the former things have passed away" *(Revelation 21:4).*

The Triune God loves the chronically ill so much, so deeply, and so self-givingly that the Word became incarnate as

Jesus Christ in order to die on their behalf and defeat the death that plagues them though their illnesses, the death that they deserved and could not defeat themselves. He did this because this is who He is. The chronically ill are not yet in their resurrection bodies — their bodies are not yet fully restored. However, God's actions in history through Jesus Christ give them full confidence that one day full healing will be their reality... This is the already-not-yet tension in which [we all] exist... the victory is already won but is not yet fully realized.

A gift the chronically ill experience is that they know in a manner that is deeper than some how valuable God's gift in Jesus Christ is. The only way for the chronically ill to be freed of the powers of death was for Christ to become incarnate, to live a perfect life, to die as a propitiation for their sins, and to be raised to life, breaking the chains of death. Such an act was the quintessential act of self-giving love...

So yes, the chronically ill experience unusual, horrible, detestable amounts of pain and suffering. We ought to hate this suffering and join with Christ in fighting against it, which the chronically ill do when they continue to press on despite their pain. However, this unusually large, horrible, detestable pain does not defeat the notion that God is love. Rather, it emphasizes all the more that God is self-giving love, and brings great hope and joy to all who hear.

AM I NORMAL?

For his spirit joins with our spirit
to affirm that we are his children.

ROMANS 8:16

If normal for a woman of my age means looking a certain way, doing predictable things at expected times, and carrying particular values close to my heart, I'm not entirely sure if I am normal or even if I *want* to be normal, but I can tell you what I *don't* want to be. Abnormal.

Being normal (or not) is all about identity, and identity is a tricky concept.

I am a daughter, mother, wife, sister, friend and co-worker. Which defines me? I value faith, a peaceful life, cooking great food, growing things outside and watching movies with my husband. Do my hobbies make me who I am?

Identity is a complex concept, one that involves culture, education, religion and many other aspects of our lives. Most of us would not want to be defined by only one relationship or interest or aspect of our being. And most of us don't want to be stuck in an identity we owned as a child or teen or during some other period in life; identity changes as we change.

Not only does the season of life we find ourselves in impact how we see ourselves, context also matters. How others perceive us affects us; the meaning society assigns to characteristics we possess is noteworthy because we will either embrace this or rebel against it.

We've all struggled, at some point, with identity; who we *want* to be clashes with what others think of us and this can trigger a range of feelings from mild annoyance to deep dismay.

I've spent years refusing to take on what some call a "disability identity." My heart condition isn't apparent to strangers and, keen to be treated normally and thought of as someone who is smart, capable and worthy of love (traits not always associated with those who are disabled) I have exerted a lot of effort trying to appear normal and denying (even to myself and the person closest to me, my husband) how much my condition impacts every moment of every day.

When you wrestle with a diagnosis or an ongoing condition it's important to know that you are not defined by what you cannot do, or by a label someone has assigned to you.

Disability affects how you experience life. You may choose to embrace a disability identity that reflects your identification with others who share a common experience: cancer survivors, those who wrestle with depression or addiction, cardiac patients... or you may not.

In the end, all Christians must come to a place where they recognize that *adoption by God* is what anchors identity.

We are who He says we are. And He says we are His beloved daughters. He chooses us. He has rescued us. He wants to be in relationship with us. We are His. This is no small thing.

There is a stigma associated with most conditions. Society values people for how strong or beautiful or rich or productive they are. And sick people, disabled people, depressed or anxious people are not always perceived as beacons of success.

Even friends and family fail to offer the kind of unconditional love we long for. Parents, spouses, children, and others we care for will not always understand us. They won't feel our pain. They can't inhabit our minds and bodies in a way that allows them to fully empathize. They have expectations, and sometimes we can't meet those expectations.

It is only in the presence of God that we find the relief that comes from being ourselves — exposing all of our brokenness — and knowing that He is not disappointed. His love doesn't waver. We are His. He has adopted us. He wants us, even when we have nothing to give.

This is a place worth settling in. Park your identity here.

Your experiences and connections, your involvements and your values influence who you are. But *center yourself* in His love. Base your identity on the price He paid for you and the unconditional love He offers you.

And I am convinced that nothing can ever separate us from God's love. Neither death nor life, neither angels nor demons, neither our fears for today nor our worries about tomorrow—not even the powers of hell can separate us from God's love. No power in the sky above or in the earth below— indeed, nothing in all creation will ever be able to separate us from the love of God that is revealed in Christ Jesus our Lord.

ROMANS 8:38-39

THOUGHTS ON THE CHALLENGE OF CEREBRAL PALSY

by Micah Carnes
(madebyacarpenter.wordpress.com)

As He passed by, He saw a man blind from birth. And His disciples asked Him, "Rabbi, who sinned, this man or his parents, that he would be born blind?" Jesus answered, *"It was* neither *that* this man sinned, nor his parents; but *it was* so that the works of God might be displayed in him. *(John 9:1-3)*

In this story, Jesus' disciples, informed by retribution theology, see a man who was born blind and they ask Jesus, "Rabbi, who sinned, this man or his parents, that he was born blind?" Jesus answered, "It was not this man that sinned, or his parents, but that **the works of God might be displayed in him**." [Emphasis added]

Now see what Jesus says here. No, the man did not sin. Nobody sinned to cause this. He was blind, he was *disabled*, to show God's works. To glorify the God of Heaven. This man was blind that Jesus might mark him and redeem him for Himself, that others might also look at his miraculous story and believe in the Lord. This man would be used to bring others into eternal life.

And why don't we go a little further? Jacob, who is representative of all believers, is interestingly *disabled* by God Himself as a way of marking Jacob as His own.

> And Jacob was left alone. And a man wrestled with him until the breaking of the day. When the man saw that he did not prevail against Jacob, **he touched his hip socket**, and **Jacob's hip was put out of joint** as he wrestled with him. Then he said, "Let me go, for the day has broken." But Jacob said, "I will not let you go unless you bless me." And he said to him, "What is your name?" And he said, "Jacob." Then he said, "Your name shall no longer be called Jacob, but Israel, **for you have striven with God and with men, and have prevailed**." Then Jacob asked him, "Please tell me your name." But he said, "Why is it that you ask my name?" **And there he blessed him**." [Emphasis added]

See what God did there? He *disabled* Jacob, and then He blessed him. God had chosen Jacob for a higher calling, just as He did the blind man. He *marked* them. When I consider these Scriptures, this is how I view my cerebral palsy. God has marked me. He is saying, "Micah, I love you and have chosen you as an instrument to spread My message to others." It would be foolish to think that this "imperfection" in my life was not already known by God. He knows it, *He created me this way,* and this is His way of saying to me that while I live in a broken world, He has marked me for His work.

To those of my readers who might also be disabled, this is how I would challenge you to think of your own disabilities. God has marked you, calling you to Himself.

PARENTING

So let's not get tired of doing what is good.
At just the right time we will reap a harvest of blessing
if we do not give up.

GALATIANS 6:9

*E*very child is unique.
My daughter's experience of my illness is interwoven with who she is, who I am, and her experience of family life in general.

I *wish* I could give my daughter every good thing and protect her from all pain, disappointment and frustration. Especially when she was young and we were adjusting to all of the sudden changes that illness imposed on our activities, I wrestled with intense guilt and deep sadness. I wanted to shop, skate, shout and stomp with her; sometimes I just wished I had the stamina to stay up late enough to manage her bedtime routine.

Those of us who struggle with illness or ongoing conditions know the extra regret that takes us beyond the usual guilt of imperfect parenting. Is it possible to parent well while being unwell? Will growing up with a parent who faces ongoing struggle damage our children?

Dwelling on the things we *can't* do is never going to bring us, or our loved ones, to a happy, healthy place. Although it may feel counter-intuitive, parents with special challenges need to be intentional about cultivating good habits and thought patterns around raising their children. Ask for help when you need it, even though you wish you could do it yourself. Don't compare yourself to your former self or to others; focus on what you *can* do and celebrate small things. Lower your standards. A fun day with mom doesn't have to mean ziplining and treetop trekking at an adventure park — why not grab some bread, drive to the lake and feed the geese together?

I struggled with this. But eventually, in spite of my longing for pre-illness stamina, I embraced a range of new activities for good days and bad ones. I acquired a fishing rod (this went nowhere — we were horrified by a hook that nearly pierced the eye of our very first catch-and-release fish), and taught my daughter piano (also a failure — every lesson ended with her wailing in a walk-in closet) — but — the point is we kept trying until we discovered new ways to spend time together.

Older parents will encounter different challenges. Children ready to leave home may have an unspoken need for reassurance that mom is going to be okay — she has rough days and lives with chronic illness, but there's no need to sacrifice life for her.

In order to release your child you may need to examine your own heart — it's natural to go through a massive period of adjustment during the empty nest stage, but women who have raised children while being ill have a special need to deal with any negative feelings that might tempt them to withhold love or withdraw emotionally in retaliation for the child's departure or absence. Your child is going to be fine, and so are you.

Many things are outside of our control. Sometimes living with illness forces us to face our own insufficiency, whereas being able-bodied offers an illusion of control. Parents who wrestle with illness *and* parents who don't must release their children into God's hands. He is the only one who knows them intimately, who loves them unconditionally, who always sees them, and who will never leave them.

Pray for your child. Connecting with a God who made the world and who loves your child more than you do is a powerful way to protect and influence them at any stage in life.

Meet
CINDY

CHALLENGES: Cancer, Pain, Fatigue

DAY TO DAY STRUGGLES

Since the age of eleven I suffered increasingly with headaches. After menopause these disappeared, but a host of other medical issues began. In my seventies, I had my uterus and ovaries removed. The year after, I had two stents put in to keep my heart working. Since then I've had a lot of shortness of breath, back-pain and sciatica pain in the right leg. At the age of seventy-nine I was diagnosed with breast cancer.

Now, ongoing back pain is an issue that keeps me from doing much of what I would like to do. Life at eighty has come down to prioritizing and doing those things that really need to be done. I was once a very active person but that is no longer so.

HOW I COPE

With the use of a walker I can walk short distances; this reduces the pain in the back and helps with balance. Tylenol has been a lifesaver to get me through the day and the night. My days are spent more and more with my husband, doing the most ordinary things such as cooking, eating, cleaning, listening to preachers, and of course spending time reading — especially reading the Bible. I am almost shocked how much I don't know about the Bible's contents, in spite of the fact that I have spent most of my adult years in Bible Studies, both leading and learning. I am so thankful that the Lord is giving me some more time to grow in my knowledge of Him.

Through the painful and difficult moments, I've been drawn closer and closer to Him, so that at times my desire truly is to go Home to my Saviour. But He obviously has a purpose for me here and He provides whatever I need from day to day. This is a lesson I've had to learn over and over again: Live one day, or even one moment, at a time.

THROUGH THE YEARS

Little by little my eyes have been opened to the truths of God's Word. Especially now, with more time on my hands I am finally learning to meditate on what life is really all about, where my hope lies and the future that is secure in my Saviour, Christ Jesus, who made it possible for me to be adopted into God's family. What an amazing miracle.

SPECIAL PEOPLE

Throughout the years, but especially at this time, I am so thankful for the encouragement of my family and friends, some giving advice on books to read and Scriptures to meditate on. Phone calls and emails from family and friends are also very helpful to get me through some days, especially connecting with my daughters.

FINAL THOUGHTS

The promise of Christ, "I will never leave you nor forsake you," needs to be my focus if I am to make it through each day. The fact of Christ's Spirit present with me at all times is also precious and something that I need to keep focused on at all times.

SELF-CARE
& SELFLESSNESS

*Each of you should use whatever gift you have received
to serve others...*
1 PETER 4:10 (NIV)

I think we're all drawn to people who give sacrificially. Mother Teresa spent her life caring for others and denying herself possessions, relationships and rest. Her writings are both inspiring and depressing — her example calls us to love like Jesus did, but this is hard to do. I can't help but feel intensely motivated *and* aware of my deep selfishness whenever I dip into her writings. Although I want to love others like she did, I don't want to give up comfort.

Does this make me selfish? Should I be willing to sacrifice *everything*, including my health, for others?

Our culture, addicted to indulgence, discourages this. Living for myself and catering to my own interests is encouraged by the media and it appeals to my sinful nature. Spoiling myself, though, is only desirable until I get carried away, forgetting how to temper or deny my impulses. Falling into a pattern of selfish behavior inevitably results in a deeply lonely and unsatisfying existence.

Still, I struggle with selfishness.

Maybe you do too.

Those of us who love Jesus would like to follow His example and obey His commands, and Jesus asks us to love others as much as we love ourselves: *Love your neighbour as yourself. (Matthew 22:36-40)*

In 1 John we read:

> Beloved, let us love one another, for love is from God; and everyone who loves is born of God and knows God. The one who does not love does not know God, for God is love. By this the love of God was manifested in us, that God has sent His only begotten Son into the world so that we might live through Him. In this is love, not that we loved God, but that He loved us and sent His Son to be the propitiation for our sins. Beloved, if God so loved us, we also ought to love one another. *1 John 4:7-11 (NASB)*

So… we have the mandate. It's intense. Jesus gave His very life in an act of sacrificial love. But how can we obey this call to love selflessly while looking after ourselves?

Although achieving balance is tricky, I believe it *is* possible (and essential) to live a life of sacrificial love while *also* practicing self-care. If I don't take care of myself, I won't be able to support others. If I develop healthy boundaries and validate the fact that I am someone *with* needs, not just someone who *meets* needs, I will have more to give.

Self-care, in the end, is a skill — one that those battling illness must develop in order to survive. Every day we make decisions that affect our health. Learning to make decisions congruent with needs dictated by a chronic condition is important if we wish to protect our health and maintain physical and emotional stability.

When I first got sick I had no idea how to do this. After all, able-bodied people don't pause to self-monitor about minor decisions. Should I eat the grape she just offered me? Do I have the stamina to walk to the mailbox? How will the heat affect my breathing? If I stay up late, what will the consequences be? Before getting sick I ate what I wanted, walked where I pleased, and generally lived each moment without much self-monitoring.

After getting sick, formerly inconsequential decisions became potential minefields. What I eat, when I eat it, how quickly I eat and what I do during digestion is very important; I now monitor myself so that decisions about food don't cause me problems. Physical exercise, ranging from a hike through the woods on a very good day, to the gentle back and forth of rubbing my husband's back on a bad day, could result in hours of arrhythmia, so I need to gauge where my body's at and proceed accordingly.

Learning to listen to my body means paying attention in moments when others plunge ahead without hesitation.

Listening to our bodies, reflecting on a range of choices and then deciding on a course of action is something we must do routinely since the stakes are high for those with chronic conditions. This is self-care, and it's essential for survival.

At the same time, self-preservation cannot be our only goal — life without love is meaningless. A life that focuses inward to the exclusion of all else is unhealthy. Trying to prolong survival while avoiding every love-rich, hope-filled, life-giving (potentially problematic) act isn't really living.

Reaching out sometimes costs us dearly, and that is okay.

We *are* called to love others sacrificially and women who face long term illness must learn to balance this with the need to protect their own health. My wellness may be my *first* priority at times, but it is not my *only* priority.

Mastering the art of balance as we love others *and* ourselves *is* possible; practicing self-care is an essential part of living selflessly since it enables us to offer the best of ourselves — emotionally and physically — to those we care about.

> *Trying to prolong survival while avoiding every love-rich, hope-filled, life-giving (potentially problematic) act isn't really living.*

PRAYER

God,

Sometimes I can hardly look after my own needs
and the thought of reaching out to help another
is overwhelming.

Give me the wisdom I need
to know when to focus on my own well being
and when to give sacrificially.

You call me to love as You love and…
Your love led You to the cross.

Lead me to quiet places
where I can bask in Your healing presence;
and give me the strength I need
to touch others with Your love.

REDEFINING GOOD

Fix your thoughts on what is true, and honorable,
and right, and pure, and lovely, and admirable.
Think about things that are excellent and worthy of praise.

PHILIPPIANS 4:8

*P*eople often ask me how I am. They've been doing this for years. Kind friends, acquaintances and family members know I have problems with my heart and thoughtfully inquire after my health.

At first I found this difficult because, to the casual observer, I was making no progress at all. I was not getting better. At six months post-op, it was becoming clear that a procedure that left me bed-ridden for over three months had not only been unsuccessful, but possibly damaging.

When my body recovered to the point where I could handle life-outside-the-bedroom, I walked at a speed more typical of people in their eighties than their thirties, and I had about half the stamina of this older group while belonging to the younger group.

People looked hopeful when they asked if I was "getting better"; I told them I was improving steadily, but very, very slowly.

I've been saying this for years.

Initially, I thought recovery would take a few days — this is what I'd been told to expect. It was a grim awakening to find that improvement came to me month by month, but definitely not day by day or even week by week.

It took years for me to work through the shock, denial, anger and dismay of suddenly losing my "normal" life; I went through a process of grieving that I'll talk more about later.

Dealing with loss is tough, and it takes time.

You may relate. Maybe anxiety prevents you from enjoying social situations you used to think nothing of. Depression makes emerging from the blissful oblivion of sleep an unwelcome and daunting chore. Physical challenges leave you exhausted after tasks that were once easy and enjoyable.

There is value in trying to be the healthiest possible version of yourself and pushing towards healing in areas where you're able to do this, but it's also important to accept the losses and limitations life thrusts on us. We can learn to redefine what having a good day looks like, and we can discipline ourselves to appreciate small joys.

For me, a steady pulse after four hours of desk work became cause to celebrate. Having the stamina to pick up groceries on the way home or to prepare a meal on a work day were things I could not do for years, so when I reached a point where I could, I felt thankful for this. I became familiar with the ebb and flow of life as someone with a condition, enjoying the good days and reminding myself, on the bad ones, that it might take a few hours, or a few days, or even a few weeks, to feel better, but not every moment would be as hard as the one I was struggling through.

I stopped comparing myself to others.

I stopped comparing myself to my former self.

I learned to discover joy in a steaming mug of tea, the warmth of a patch of sunlight on my skin, the voice of my mother in my ear. What gives *you* pleasure? What fills you with hope? Does anything delight you? *I* relish crisp autumn air, the pump of blood in my legs — the joy of physical exertion on exceptionally good days. *You* can learn, as I have, to savour those things that are uniquely life-giving to your soul. Redefine good, explore new possibilities and cherish sweet moments.

Meet
DONNA

CHALLENGE

I was born with a condition known as spina bifida. To keep it simple, spina bifida is a birth defect that occurs when the spine and spinal cord do not form properly; it is a type of neural tube defect. Spina bifida can be very severe, somewhat severe or very mild. I would classify mine as somewhat severe. I have a certain degree of paralysis, particularly in the back of my body and legs, which has affected my walking ability and certain bodily functions have been impaired. My brother, who was five years older than me, was born with severe spina bifida and he passed away two weeks after his birth.

A BIT ABOUT ME

I grew up in the Kawartha Lakes area and I now live in Barrie. I have been married, and I have a forty-two-year-old son who lives in San Diego, California. He does not have spina bifida. I have been blessed to be able to work in the mental health field for thirty years.

STRUGGLES

I would not be truthful if I did not admit that there have been challenges with this disability. I have been at the Sick Children's Hospital and St. Michael's Hospital in Toronto many times for surgeries on my legs. Most of these surgeries were when I was a young child, although later there were more operations in an attempt to keep me ambulatory.

These surgeries allowed me to walk for more than fifty years. I am still able to be active and to participate in so many of life's pleasures. For much of the past twenty years, I have been in a wheelchair and this has made things easier for me as I was having so much difficulty with having enough balance to keep walking.

HOW I COPE

What has allowed me to transition through the various challenges of this disability is my walk with Jesus. This was not totally present in my younger life. By opening my heart to Jesus, I have not been able to avoid the trials that have been given to me, but He sure has lightened this journey for me. Some have questioned me about how I can have faith in light of such challenges. To this I respond that I serve a God who gives me peace that passes all understanding. When my trials have been the heaviest, God has been there with me to give me the peace that I have needed. He has carried me through so much brokenness and pain. He has been there to pull me from darkness to light.

SPECIAL PEOPLE

I was fortunate to be born into a supportive and loving family. I was the only living child, and they taught me to persevere and be positive in the face of adversity. I was made to believe, from an early age, that my disability need not hold me back. God gave me a mother who just pushed me to accomplish things that I may otherwise never have attempted in my lifetime. My mother was such a strong woman who spent her life supporting me. God did not save my marriage, but He gave me a son who continues to infuse my life with such joy. His magnificent sense of humor has carried both of us through some very tough times.

LAST THOUGHTS

This disability has not been a significant burden to me. Yes, there have been some challenges all along the way, but they have never defined who I was meant to be. Ultimately, God has determined my identity as His child.

CRISIS

You have been my refuge,
a place of safety when I am in distress.
PSALM 59:16

*O*ne morning I woke with a wonderful sense of well-being. My body felt warm and I was caught in that lovely, drowsy state between sleep and consciousness. All was serene in my world until I realized that I was not in my bed; my six-foot frame was stretched out across the hardwood landing of our upstairs hall. How did I get here?

It came back to me in moments. I'd gone to bed in the middle of an episode of arrhythmia; often these episodes resolve in sleep as my breathing slows and my body rhythms calm, but this time when I woke to use the bathroom, my heart was still intensely erratic. I stood up too quickly, and as I left the room, the lack of oxygen caused me to misjudge my movements — I went full speed ahead into the wall, ricocheted off of it, slammed into the hall wall behind me and slid down to the floor, where I lost consciousness.

Crisis interrupts the gentle, predictable rhythm of my life more often than I care to admit.

I think of myself as a calm person. I live a quiet life — boring, perhaps, but pleasantly predictable. I'm a free spirit, really, but I like to enjoy spontaneity *after* I've hung up my pyjamas, taken a shower, combed my hair in the same way as always, and made an egg with toast for breakfast. Routine makes me feel safe and helps me to stay emotionally even — as in stress-free — which is good for my very temperamental heart.

Others see me as Holly, the calm one. Very little ruffles my feathers. On the outside. But on the inside, I go through crisis at least once a month — sometimes more. And this is harrowing.

Maybe you relate.

I won't bore you with the details of what it feels like when horrible physical sensations shake up every part of my body, from my bowels to my toes, draining my strength and leaving me like a limp, discarded hanky when the dust finally settles. But I will say that each time I go through this, the internal me that I hide from others experiences all of the hallmarks of a crisis: lowered ability to concentrate, difficulty with abstract thought, irritability, feelings that are unpredictable, the impulse to withdraw from others, extreme sensitivity to external stimulation, fear, dismay, a sense of hopelessness and helplessness.

I suspect I am not alone. Perhaps you succumb to panic attacks. Or maybe extreme pain interferes with your life. I know one woman who experiences paralysis in response to temperature changes. This kind of trauma, this kind of crisis, becomes routine for some who live with illness. In spite of this, crisis is never normal, nor, in my experience, is it possible to escape the emotional toll that acute distress causes. There are a few lessons I've learned, though, that help me to minimize the damaging impact of each crisis that visits me.

Perhaps the biggest revelation, over the years, has been the realization that making big decisions during moments of crisis is a bad idea. We all know this. Who hasn't heard, after someone close to us loses a loved one, that life changes should be put on hold for a while? I've discovered that when I'm in the grip of a crisis or its aftermath, this is not the time to sort out my feelings about work, marriage, parenting or any other significant aspect of life. This is a moment to set aside complex discussion and thought. This is an occasion to seek comfort.

What comforts you? Quiet jazz? Hot chocolate in a familiar mug? An eighties comedy? Treat yourself with the same soothing attentiveness you would show to a distressed child. Does anyone propel a child, fresh out of a justified meltdown, back into the day's routine without a word of reassurance, a hug, or a treat? The best parents rub the child's back, smooth her hair and speak gently to her until that fresh sense of distress is muted by the loudness of their reassurance.

But, you say, *there is no one here to rub my back, to tell me everything will be okay, to say he will take care of me.* **No one knows.**

You are mistaken. God knows. Climb into His lap during these moments — turn your face towards His and allow Him to restore your balance. Settle in His arms. Let Him be your place of safety during times of distress. Many of the women who share their stories in this book mention the comfort they have drawn from reading Psalms, listening to worship music or hearing reassurance from God through scripture. These women don't always feel God's nearness, but they know what to do to cultivate an awareness of His presence in themselves. And they do this intentionally, knowing that their overall well-being is improved when they place themselves in God's arms, resting in the truth that when they are too weak to hang on, He will not let go.

Meet
ANTJE

CHALLENGES: Post-Polio Syndrome, Fibromyalgia, Crippled Right Foot

DAY TO DAY STRUGGLES

Fibromyalgia has been a big issue; I've heard someone say it's like a buffet, and this is true — it affects so many things in your whole body. I never know how this will affect me; it might be IBS or it could be headaches, or maybe something else. Also, muscle atrophy, joint pain and difficulty walking have gotten worse as I age; my main challenge now is my right foot, which is crippled from the polio. I've had to use crutches for the past twenty-two years. This first started when I was only fifty-four and at first I was very depressed about having to use crutches to walk... but I got used to it.

EARLY DAYS

I was born and grew up in Germany. My family was not the church-going kind. We believed in God and called ourselves Christians; after all, we lived a good life and did nothing terrible like murder or such, so we must be alright.

GOD WAS ALWAYS THERE

Through a number of events in my life: polio as a child, the after-effects of the disease, coming to Canada, getting married and having two children... God was always there to guide me and to protect me... I just did not know it!

JOURNEY TO GOD

My parents came to Canada from Germany for a visit and while here my father died suddenly. Through the shock and grief, the thought came to me: *This can't be all; life goes on after this.* And so, my journey towards God began. One night, feeling very low, I prayed "Jesus, if you are real, show me." He did!

FAVOURITE HYMN

The hymn *Amazing Grace* will always be special to me. Hearing it for the first time opened my eyes and my heart. It assured me of my salvation: *I once was lost, but now I am found, was blind but now I see.* Here I was, born again, a brand new life, full of joy. But there was so much to learn (and there still is). As time went by there were trials, sickness and sins... mine and those of others. This brought pain and sorrow.

WITHOUT GOD I WOULD BE LOST

Some years ago I went through a dark night of the soul. I had chest pains, palpitations and felt intense anxiety. Then the head pain started. Day and night I had severe pain, like nerve pain, in my head and it went on and on. Doctors tried drug after drug, but nothing helped. On the contrary, the drugs affected me in a negative way. I had extreme anxiety; I felt like I wanted to jump out of my body. I had difficulty eating and lost twenty pounds. I couldn't sleep at night and I couldn't stand being alone in the house. I wasn't suicidal, but I was just so tired of living; I really didn't feel I wanted to live anymore.

HOW I COPED

God sustained me. Reading the Psalms really encouraged me. Also, it was during that time that I began journaling, and whenever I'm going through a bad time now, I look back and feel reassured that *this too shall pass.* Many times God encouraged me through scripture, songs and Christian friends, but I also found it necessary to take care of myself by exercising regularly (I swim three times a week), and watching what I eat. When I look back there were so many times when God just came and sat with me — I don't always feel close to Him, but I know He's always there. Without God I would be lost.

LAST THOUGHTS

Jesus promised to never leave us or forsake us. And He never will. *Through many dangers, toils and snares I have already come. T'was Grace that brought me safe thus far and Grace will lead me home.*

THE GREAT BEYOND

*Therefore we do not lose heart. Though outwardly
we are wasting away, yet inwardly we are being renewed day by day.
For our light and momentary troubles are achieving for us
an eternal glory that far outweighs them all. So we fix our eyes not
on what is seen, but on what is unseen. For what is seen
is temporary, but what is unseen is eternal.*
2 CORINTHIANS 4:16-18 (NASB)

*F*ear of death is a really personal issue — it's rooted in our beliefs and life experiences and I'm not sure it's possible for one person to coach another into a place of peace about it. I want to share my own experience, though, in the hope that, in some way, it encourages you.

It wasn't until my symptoms became serious that I began to see death as a real possibility; when an important organ in your body begins to malfunction, it's natural to think about mortality.

A lot of people believe they'll go to heaven when they die, but they still seem uncertain and scared when death draws near. I understand, but I don't share those feelings.

Faith has always been very important to me, and God a real part of life. My most delightful moments have been contemplative times when I felt a spiritual connection with God. There is a sweetness in the memory of these moments that is far better than any earthly pleasure I've experienced, and, for me, moving into eternity means moving towards that sweetness: the presence of God.

Still, thinking about death doesn't only mean facing what comes after. For some it involves reflecting on the long-term effects of illness — the unpleasant journey ahead. For me death involves leaving behind precious people, so I wrestle with fears about how loss will affect them.

I struggled with this a lot in the early days of my diagnosis. My daughter was still young in those days, and I wondered who would braid her hair each morning if I died. Who would kiss my husband's cheek or tell him how sweet he is?

How can You ask me to leave them behind? How can You let this happen?

I threw this question at God. Angry. Frustrated. Fearful.

And an answer came to me — a quiet sense of His view of things. *I love them more than you do. I have a plan for their good. I will not allow you to be taken from them without having a plan for their good and their care.*

His answer settled my angst and I bring it to mind whenever fear returns to grip me.

Sometimes I lie in bed with pain in my heart, literally and figuratively. I wonder what lies ahead. Will I outlive everyone, my flawed heart doing a surprisingly satisfactory job of keeping me alive?

Or will I slip into that other place... the place that was created by the One who knows my deepest longings and joys, the One who invented the sweetest pleasures I've found here on Earth, who is eager to grasp my hand and tug me into a deeper experience of His creative expressions — there — in the Great Beyond?

I'd rather stay. I have to be honest. This world is familiar and there's a lot I still want to do. There are loved ones I'm reluctant to leave behind.

In any event, an uncertain future has made me realize something. **Neither you nor I know the hour we will leave this place. It could be soon, or we may have many years yet.**

I am sure you know of people taken unexpectedly, without a moment's notice. It could be like that for me, or for you or for anyone else we know. We're not so different from others, you and I.

All of us are fragile. Our bodies are breakable.

But our spirits are eternal. And the health of the spirit is very much within our grasp. We can have a strong, clean spirit if we want to.

I encourage you to make a decision that will give you a sense of control in spite of the physical or emotional limitations you face.

Strive to have the healthiest spirit possible.

Set your heart on things above, not on earthly things.

Bask in your identity as someone rescued, adopted and loved by God. And when it is your turn to move from this life to the next, whether this is soon or a long way off, the transition will be a serene one because your spirit is strong, your identity is grounded in spiritual truth, and you leave this place in love with the One you're going to see, knowing that He holds you and the ones you love tightly in His hand.

PRAYER

Creator of All,
You were here before I was born and
You will be here when I am gone.
You urge me to value unseen things above the physical;
help me to live as though I believe that this temporary life
is only the prelude to an eternity with You.
Comfort me when I fear the unknown
of what the future holds for my loved ones
and for me.
I trust in Your unfailing love.
Amen.

LOSS

God blesses those who mourn, for they will be comforted.
MATTHEW 5:4

*T*hose who wrestle with ongoing conditions, or who suddenly get seriously ill, face loss.

For me losing the ability to run, jump or shout without risking an episode was depressing. After decades of romping through life — racing through dorm halls at breakneck speed, dangling upside down from tree branches, trying out alpine skiing and belly dancing and basketball... I had to stop.

Relational losses followed closely on the heels of my physical decline. The need to protect my own wellness meant setting boundaries that others didn't always like or understand. Changes in what I could do and how I could express myself created a shift in the tone of my interactions with those closest to me. I could no longer go skating or biking with my daughter. I couldn't stay up late with my husband. I hated this. It made me feel guilty and frustrated.

Although *ambiguous loss* is a term most often used to describe the trauma faced by relatives of those who suffer neural damage or dementia-type decline, it's an idea that can also be helpful to those of us struggling with other types of loss. Life is not the same as it was before. A chronic condition may have left you or a loved one searching for answers. You may lack the sense of closure that we long for when letting go of something precious. Becoming familiar with the concept of ambiguous loss can be helpful for those struggling to process or articulate ongoing changes caused by illness.

Like me, you may recognize one common after-effect of loss in your own life — splitting your history into two sections: **before** and **after**. Before you were diagnosed, and after. Before the onset of symptoms, and after. People who do this are reacting to trauma of some kind. An incident, a diagnosis, or the onset of illness has altered life so severely that this new season seems completely different from all that preceded it.

In all cases, grieving loss in a healthy way means allowing ourselves to fully recognize and mourn what we've lost — a way of life, relationships, finances, a future we dreamed of. Actively allowing ourselves to acknowledge and mourn these losses takes work and it takes courage. For some it means seeking therapy, or working through a self-guided course or book.

You may feel tempted to downplay the impact of a diagnosis in your life, or you may avoid dealing with grief. It can hurt to think about the waves of consequences one significant loss has brought to your life; mourning is painful.

What none of us deserves, though, is to get stuck in a place where those initial emotions of anger, denial, shock and depression continue to dominate. Living with chronic illness is hard enough without stagnating in a bad place. The goal, for us, is to move through a healthy grieving process to a place of resilience and hope, a place where it's possible to **celebrate what remains** and to discover **new hope** for the future.

Meet
SARAH

CHALLENGES: Fibromyalgia, Chronic Depression, Arthritis

DAY TO DAY STRUGGLES

My fibromyalgia and arthritis pain symptoms are usually fairly mild. I do experience pain, but more often it is the sensation of my body being weighed down as if by wet cement. It is hard to explain. I think because depression is common with fibromyalgia, it is difficult to be entirely clear about what I am experiencing or feeling. But the weariness and sense of moving through wet cement is not merely physical — even my thoughts feel weighed down and sludge like.

ABOUT DEPRESSION

I have experienced grief, but my experience of depression is a different kind of sadness. It is dull and bland and dark — sometimes it makes me feel feelingless. I don't produce enough of a certain chemical for my brain. I take medication and it helps me a great deal. My doctor gave me a helpful image about chronic depression. She described life and the things it holds as a big pile of hay. We stand in the field and pitch the hay and deal with it one fork load at a time. However, when someone suffers from chronic depression because of hormone or chemical imbalance, instead of standing on the field pitching their pile of hay, it is like they are standing in a hole. Sometimes they can reach the pile, but it is hard and uses a great deal of energy. Sometimes they can't reach the pile very well at all. Medication will not deal with my pile of hay (some people may need extra help with that — therapy or counseling), but it puts me on the field.

FEAR OF A FATAL OUTCOME

I also experience some stress reactions related to trauma. We lost our first born, Anna Pearl, when she was three months old. She had a significant heart defect, but her prognosis was quite positive and so her death was unexpected. It was also physically traumatic. The Lord was gracious to us and we can truly say that we have acceptance and can even see good that God did through our loss. However, I continue to experience involuntary reactions of dread and fear when my two (healthy and active) sons are injured or sick. It is as though a channel was carved in my brain when Anna Pearl died and certain things cause my mind to slip into that channel. The channel could be labeled "expectation of a fatal outcome." I am aware of this channel and I can usually remind myself that this is not necessarily a rational reaction. But I cannot seem to prevent my mind from slipping into that channel in the first place.

WHY DO I FEEL WHAT I FEEL?

I find that the difficulty lies in the invisibleness of it all. I feel I must discern myself whether I am weary because of my chronic condition or because I am being lazy or because I am carrying a spiritual burden. Am I sad because of chemical imbalances in my brain or because of an issue or circumstance I should process? Or is it because I am facing some kind of spiritual opposition? Should I have a nap or should I push through? Should I explore the dark feelings to resolve them or should I turn away from them? Do I need a refuge or a rebuke? I can't possibly figure it out myself all the time. I find this emotionally exhausting.

HOW I COPE

Music is powerful for helping me out of a spiral of unnecessary self-scrutiny. Also, there are a number of verses and truths in Scripture that have become like stabilizers for me.

"For He Himself knows our form; He is mindful that we are nothing but dust." Psalm 103:14 (NASB)

God knows my frame. I remember sitting in a classroom in rural Kenya feeling discouraged; the children were not co-operating and it had been a rough day of teaching. Filling the view through the open window was Mt. Makuli, a vision of beauty and strength. Some of the mountain was covered in lush, green vegetation, but parts of it were scraped of its green and left with craggy places of rich red soil — or, in some places, gleaming bare rock. I remember the Lord gently teaching me that He created both the lush parts and the scraped away parts to give the breath-taking glory of that mountain. It would not be so awesome if it were all green foliage. He comforted me that He knew exactly how much pressure to apply and what to scrape away in my life so that both soft, easy parts and painful, wounding parts could result in good. The comfort is that He knows my frame, and He is not surprised when I feel as unsubstantial as dust. The wonder is that somehow the scraping and wounding could result in glory.

In *Genesis 16:13* it says of Hagar, the slave of Abraham, "She gave this name to the LORD who spoke to her: "You are the God who sees me." *(NIV)* I find this so securing. God sees me. **Sometimes I just pray that over and over: *"Lord you see me."*** He sees my day, the particular weakness I am feeling — the reality of it and the experience of it. He can bring clarity.

I also like the story of Elijah; he experiences a tremendous victory and miracle, but then falls into a terrible despondency. He asks God to let him die. The Lord sends an angel who tells him to eat his supper. The Lord was gentle with Elijah and had him do the next needful thing — a basic life responsibility, or need. Sometimes if I am in a slump my husband will gently say, *"Go make your supper,"* a reminder to do some simple, needful task (cooking or perhaps folding the laundry or emptying the dishwasher). Often this moves me to the next thing, and the next thing.

FINAL THOUGHTS

My days begin in need. I have two strong, active boys who need a hearty breakfast. And I homeschool them, so they also need a teacher. Some mornings it feels as though I am beginning the day already depleted of strength. I lie in bed and pray and pray: *"Jesus, I need your strength. Jesus, please help me to get up."* I would rather He miraculously lift my body and infuse it with a tangible electric charge of sudden energy, but usually getting up is a step of faith. I have to step out onto the floor of my bedroom and then take another step, and another. Even if I have no energy, I find His strength is there.

I have come to the understanding that in a dreadful but wonderful way all my prayers for strength are prayers for my own weakness. The Lord has promised that His strength is made perfect in weakness. I desperately want God's strength because it is wise, patient, loving and enduring. But if that strength is most perfectly experienced in weakness, then to pray for it is a prayer for emptying, a request for my weakness to be a locus for the experience of God's strength. I believe when we try to disguise or hide our weakness, we hide from ourselves and others the glory of God in our lives.

My physical and emotional weaknesses, my broken, limping parts, are grim reminders of the fallen state of our world. However, God's power and His good purposes in and for my brokenness are wonder-full.

TRIBE

He comforts us in all our troubles so that we can comfort others.
When they are troubled, we will be able to give them
the same comfort God has given us.

2 CORINTHIANS 1:4

*T*here is something about reading the words of another person who has faced extreme physical difficulty that is startlingly encouraging. When I first got sick I read books like *Lessons I Learned in the Dark* by Jennifer Rothschild, who went blind in her youth, and the biography of Joni Eareckson Tada, who lost the use of much of her body after a diving accident.

I allowed these writers to pull me into their thoughts and experiences. Words written by women who had experienced sudden losses greater than mine comforted and challenged me; Joni and Jennifer embraced life after loss with strength and purpose. Reading their books enabled me to intentionally cultivate in myself a sense of gratitude for the good things I enjoyed each day. Also, at a time when I was still in shock over my sudden loss of abilities, dipping into books by disabled authors made me feel understood. They'd gone through this too. I was not as alone as I thought.

Although I don't know anyone, at the moment, who shares my diagnosis, through the years I've bumped into a few people with symptoms similar to mine.

I felt a surprising kinship with one church acquaintance waiting for a heart transplant — this man and I had little in common, but when he confessed that walking from his car to the front door made his heart race as though he'd sprinted the whole way, I understood.

Another woman shared with me, soon after we were introduced, that often after a day-long episode of arrhythmia she felt so weak she could barely make it to the bathroom. This woman's name was Grace — my grandmother's name — and she seemed beautiful to me; she embodied grace. She was kind, warm and open. Her words touched a hurting, lonely place in my soul. She understood.

Adjusting to loss, to a diagnosis or condition that radically alters life, is disorienting, and I found the first years of this process tough. At that time, I yearned to connect with others who had experienced what I was going through. Could anyone reassure me? Understand me? Rescue me?

As the years passed, I learned to listen. I found people who understood me in the seniors who told me how hard it was for them to walk without assistance, and in post-op swimmers doing lengths at the pool. I began to realize that, all around me, people suffered. Life brings loss. That loss doesn't look the same for everyone — but real people face pain in their lives, and they struggle with this. There are more of us than you might think.

I once met a little girl who lingered at the customer service desk where I worked, staring at me oddly.

"Nice new glasses," I said.

No, she informed me, the glasses were not new.

Her teenage brother urged her to move along, but she refused, saying she needed to show me something. She unzipped her winter jacket and I obligingly exclaimed over her pink, frilly shirt.

No, she said again, not the shirt.

She lifted the pink fabric and I grew uncomfortable. What did she want me to see?

She drew my attention to a lump in her shirt.

"She wants to show you her heart monitor," her brother told me.

A heart monitor!

I felt an instant bond with this child. We chatted, our heads close together, about the discomfort of having those sticky black tabs adhered to the skin, and the trouble of not being allowed to bathe, and the oddness of having wires twisting around your torso.

That child became an instant friend.

———————————

Suffering and shared experience draw us together. I know that pain can be lonely, that loss can cause us to feel isolated in our unique experience of grief. Sometimes we have to mourn on our own for a while. But, when we're ready, just outside the door is a community of others who struggle. Glossy ads may trick us into feeling as though we're the only ones with a weird life — no one we know is as depressed or anxious or weak or incapable as we are. But believe me, loss is almost universal. We are strongest when we support one another. Listen for the undertones in what people share — the mention of a child's name, the tight lips as someone talks about an ex-spouse, the shine of fear with the mention of a trip to the doctor.

As someone who suffers, you have something special to give. You can listen with understanding and act with compassion; you can recognize in others your own suffering, feeling their pain and relieving some of it simply by listening well and belonging, as they do, to a tribe of real women who struggle.

Meet
BERTHA

CHALLENGES: Anxiety, Depression

IN THE BEGINNING

My youngest brother was killed in a car accident at the age of thirty-two, leaving behind three little girls and an unborn baby. Five years later, my father was diagnosed with stage four cancer; he died four months after his diagnosis. Shortly after the first tragic, life-changing event I went into early menopause; I was in my late thirties and didn't have a clue what to do or what was happening to me. It was a very, very difficult time.

DAY TO DAY STRUGGLES

Physically, my condition can exhaust me. I feel so sad or tired or angry — it hits quietly and then takes over. Inner voices tear me down, saying *you're a failure; you're incompetent*. I cry a lot and it's almost worse than mourning, because when you mourn you know why, but when you're depressed you don't.

ABOUT RELATIONSHIPS

For a time, I gave up on some relationships — I just felt so numb, I didn't have the ability to be the friend I thought I should be. I also found that some people were just draining — my head would spin and I just couldn't handle the pressure of their issues. I like people; I am very social, so this was difficult for me… but I had to give myself permission to step back so that I could get better.

HOW I COPE

I really try to live in the moment — if I don't, things spiral out of control, my stress builds, and I can't function very well. I pray without ceasing, worship, and I read and hide scripture in my heart. I have tried memorizing scripture so that in the middle of the night, if I awaken, I can quote a verse or two. This comforts me on those sometimes long nights.

MY LIFE VERSE

Trust in the LORD with all your heart and do not lean on your own understanding. In all your ways acknowledge Him and He will make your paths straight. *Proverbs 3:5-6 (NASB)*

SPECIAL PEOPLE

My parents' example of faith and unconditional love are still with me today, and my husband, Greg, has walked with me even in the darkest times — his love and support have helped me immensely. My two children have also been such a source of strength — I am so blessed to have them in my life. Also, those who are closest to me among my family and friends know who they are; we've had many discussions and I have even asked for forgiveness — this really lifted any burden I might have carried. I am eternally grateful.

LAST THOUGHTS

This battle has brought me closer to God as I have truly had to rely on His strength. I thought this journey would end in time, but it hasn't, so I realize that God really does want all my attention and trust! I would just like to say that **storms will come**. It's how we are prepared to handle them that matters.

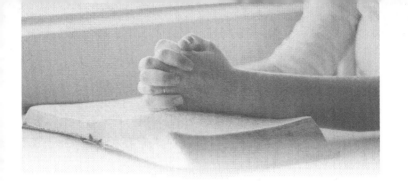

USE ME TODAY

The helpless put their trust in you.

PSALM 10:14

I always hope for a good day.

Unlike my younger days, when waking up was synonymous with throwing back the covers and launching my body into an upright position, these days moving out of sleep must be done like everything else — with utmost caution! Asking my heart to shift gears always signifies potential trouble and waking up is one of the hardest things I do each day. Sometimes I need to let my mind kick into action for a while before moving any part of my body. Other days, exposure to light has to be carefully gradual.

Regardless, even on mornings when my heart seems extra-temperamental, I hope for good things and mentally frame the day in a context that forces positive expectation. Sometimes I ask God for a symptom-free day, and sometimes I don't.

God says He hears when I pray, but He does not always answer the way I want Him to. One way I protect my relationship with God is by praying often about things that do not relate to my physical condition. Hope cannot be solely about physical healing or wellness.

Prayer is a touchy topic for me. It's easy to become disillusioned and consequently to avoid conversing with a God who listens, but who does not do what I ask Him to do. Because of this I need to remind myself often that God is looking at a bigger picture than I am. He is not inclined, as I am, to forget that spiritual realities impact eternity, whereas the physical is fleeting.

Sometimes I think prayer should be easier than it is. Talking to my husband is a joy. Chatting with my daughter is delightful. Why isn't communicating with my Creator like this? I find prayer hard.

This, I think, is due to two flaws in how I think of and approach talking to God.

First, I assume prayer is an innate ability, easy for all believers (except me) — but it's not. Like communication in any relationship, prayer is a skill that must be learned. It takes perseverance to establish good habits in our relationships with people and it takes persistent intention to establish good habits in our relationship with God.

Second, I often slip into the mistake of centering my prayer life around my emotional and physical needs. A richer, more satisfying spiritual life is possible if I shift the focus away from what I want and if I remember that Jesus is the answer to my deepest needs. There *is* hope. I *have been* rescued.

Two practices help me as I battle my natural inclination to avoid prayer: abiding and listening for His call. Maybe they can help you, too.

ABIDE

Spend time abiding in God's presence. This looks different for each person — it may mean getting outside and contemplating nature. It could involve memorizing scripture or listening to worshipful music. Whatever stirs you, opening your spirit to God's presence — do this. Make this a priority. When I intentionally cultivate an awareness of God's nearness, this sweetens all of life.

LISTEN FOR HIS CALL

God has a mission for you. You're not here just for you, and you're not here just to endure the misery of a difficult life until He finally calls you Home. How does God want to use you? No idea? Ask Him. Listen for a reply. If you don't hear anything, spend time meditating on your gifting — those abilities He's given you. Think about needs that you're aware of. Is He calling you to intercede for others on days that you spend in bed? Might He ask you to text, email or snail mail others, forging connections and lifting spirits as you do? Or is there something else? Read scripture — look up all those exciting verses that reveal God's heart for the broken, the needy, and for those who are suffering injustice. Has He placed a burden on your heart for a specific category of people? How can you reach out *today*?

YOU HAVE A FUTURE AND IT BEGINS TODAY

As we sat around the dining table, discussing my husband's cold symptoms, our conversation went where everyone's thoughts go these days when someone gets sick: *What if it's COVID-19*? I made an offhand comment about how lonely I would be if both my husband and daughter died, leaving me behind. My husband's response took me by surprise and shook me into a new view of life.

I was thinking about the future as a lengthy ordeal to struggle through. I often do. Many of my dreams aren't attainable anymore. There are so many physically intense activities I'd love to engage in… but my existence is subdued. Limited. So, yes, without realizing it, I guess I often frame my remaining years here as a kind of long wait.

My husband, in his direct and articulate way, told me to enjoy the time I have. Use it. It'll pass so quickly. Don't just endure it.

Is the most significant season of my life over? Or is God powerful enough to show up in a future that begins with today?

His gentle rebuke shook me out of something bigger than my offhand comment about hypothetical loneliness. It reminded me that life is not over until it's over. Our time here is a gift.

Do we believe God when He says that He delights in using the weak to confound the wise? Do I believe that His power is made perfect in my weakness? Is the most significant season of my life over? Or is God powerful enough to show up in a future that begins with today?

———————————

PRAYER

God,
Sometimes I am angry with You
for allowing loss to take so much from me.
Is there anything left in my life… in me…
that You can still use?
Your Word contains countless examples
of ruined lives and ruined people
loved and used by You.
I believe that You love me,
that You weep over my loss,
that You will use me in spite of my weakness.
I trust You.
Amen.

REMEMBERING

As my life was slipping away
I remembered the LORD.
JONAH 2:7

*Y*ears ago I quit my job. It was foolish. I supported the family at that time and this job paid well, with full time, flexible hours. Yet, I'd realized that to stay in this workplace meant compromising my integrity. So I quit. And, scary as that was, this act ushered me into a rare place in my walk of faith. I did something for God and it cost me and I sensed the presence of God almost tangibly that day in our shabby living room. This was not a mundane moment in my life of faith. *Would I obey? Even if it cost us our livelihood?*

God provided, that day. Half an hour after quitting my job our phone rang: a job offer.

God. Undeniably God.

Some days I forget. My spiritual life feels dull. Routine. Prayer is as ordinary as scraping compost into the bin. A healthy practice, but very humdrum.

Let me take you back with me, to one more memory.

Preaching may have stirred me more often in years gone by, but it rarely moved me to tears. Barely finished college, I sat in my rented room watching an old VHS recording of a preacher who became more and more animated as he talked about walking with God all our days. His passion roused my own, and although I'd seen this video before, I wept as the preacher recited the words of a hymn I would usually find dated and dull: *I come to the garden alone, while the dew is still on the roses... and He walks with me and He talks with me and He tells me I am His own, and the joy we share as we tarry there, none other has ever known.*

I cried. I felt it. Could it be true, that God felt this joy, too? Did He love moments with me as much as I loved moments with Him? I longed for it to be so. I longed for love. But I doubted. I wasn't sure.

Later that same week I met with my spiritual mentor, a wise older woman. We prayed together and spent some time in silence and she held up her hands and said the Lord was sharing something with her. Then she hummed the tune and said the words: *And He walks with me and He talks with me and He tells me I am His own... and the joy we share as we tarry there, none other has ever known.*

I'd told no one. I was shy about feelings and cautious in sharing, and devotional times were personal. Passion was personal. I didn't tell her why God might be sharing that song with her. But I treasured this in my heart — a miraculous affirmation of God's love for me. And I remembered it, for years after.

That bloom we feel, when God shows up in an extraordinary way, fades. We forget.

Aware of this tendency, God fills His word with the admonition to remember. *Remember* Him when we're on our beds, *remember* His name, *remember* the Sabbath, *remember* the days of old, *do this* to remember.

It's a mistake to think we can live on a spiritual high all the time. No part of life is like that. The hardest moments and the boring moments may cause us to wonder about God's presence in our lives; we may doubt our own spiritual strength or value. These feelings are a normal part of our journey — life brings us highs and lows. Spiritual life is no different. Carry yourself through these times with two practices.

First, remember that the truth about who God is, who we are, and our commitment to Him does not change just because our feelings are all over the place. Keep a list of things you know for sure —

statements of truth about your identity as a woman who is deeply loved by the Creator of the world.

Second, build into your life a practice of remembering times when God showed up. Give thanks. And allow the memory of mountaintop moments to sustain you in the valleys.

WE ARE WEAK
BUT HE IS STRONG

When I am afraid
I will put my trust in You.
PSALM 56:3

Sometimes illness creeps into your life gradually and other times it slams into you with a storm that is sudden, unexpected and loud.

I went through a gradual realization — years of diagnostic appointments followed by the fumbling discomfort of a young doctor sharing my diagnosis with me. Later, I suffered the sudden shock of a failed attempt at intervention. It seemed to me, then, that no one I knew was sick. No one could understand.

Gradually I realized that there are different kinds of suffering and that a steady diet of the wrong kind of media had skewed my perception of reality. I was not abnormal. Everyone else was not healthy, happy and able-bodied. People all around me struggled.

Writing this book opened my eyes further to a community of women who wrestle with deep physical and emotional issues. I don't like thinking about my condition or its impact. Even as my body is taken over by sensations that are horrible and intense, I prefer to have a "normal" day, interacting as usual and focusing on other things. Because of this I felt resistant to the idea of sharing my story with you — **I did not want to write this book** because the project forced me to spend hours thinking about things I'd rather forget.

But I don't regret it. I want God to use my unfinished story of ongoing brokenness to encourage others. The unconditional love and hope God has brought to the situation that is my imperfect and broken life He can also bring to yours.

The Bible is filled with stories of messy lives and less than heroic people. Sometimes we make the mistake of revering renowned biblical figures, forgetting the brokenness that runs, interrupted only by Jesus, through scripture. We lose sight of the overall plot — the mission — the sweep of the Bible. This book doesn't exist to document the historical feats of people who lived long ago; it exists to document *God's* story. He redeems the situation — again and again. He does this in the lives of Bible characters and He does it in my life. In the end, writing this book didn't force me to spend hours thinking about symptoms and losses — it caused me to spend hours dwelling on God's faithfulness to me and to women I know.

I encourage you to be brave and to share your possibly unresolved, still-less-than-ideal story with someone else. It is very likely that doing so will lessen the loneliness of the person you open up with because knowing that someone else feels anguish and fear can be incredibly comforting.

If you know God and have experienced His comfort as you've fought your way through years of anxiety or depression or pain or addiction, God can use your story and suffering in profound ways. After all, isn't the essence of God's story His persistence in reaching into our broken world and our imperfect lives with a hand that offers to rescue us and to provide us with what we long for most?

Unfailing love.

A future.

Hope.

ACKNOWLEDGEMENTS

My heartfelt gratitude goes out to the women
in my Bible study and church.
Your honesty has helped me to realize
that we all struggle,
and your warm support after the release of my first book
gave me the courage to write again.

I also want to thank Lynn, Brooke and Andrea
for offering their services as editors.

Thank you to each woman who contributed to this book.
Reading your stories touched and inspired me.

My sister, Kerry, transformed an ugly Word document
into this beautiful book.
Kerry, you must be the most patient
and talented graphic designer out there.
Thank you for helping me.

I wrote this book for my husband, Alexis,
who has suffered with me
and loved me through a lot of loss.
I love you.

If you enjoyed this book, would you consider helping me to share it with others by rating or reviewing it online or sharing it on social media?

Visit me at www.hollydicksonramos.com

Manufactured by Amazon.ca
Bolton, ON